Ethan's wings

A mother's journey of faith

———————————

KiKi Jones

Published in the United States by ETHANS WINGS PUBLISHING

ETHAN'S WINGS: A MOTHER'S JOURNEY OF FAITH

ISBN-1502369699
ISBN13:978-1502369697

ETHAN'S WINGS

Dedication

I pray that my heavenly angel Ethan has had time to spread his wings. Not a day goes by that he is not thought about or missed. Rest my sweet angel knowing that I love you.

This book is dedicated to all the angels that have left us too soon leaving family and friends to mend broken pieces. This book is also dedicated to the many moms whose stories go untold, but the pain remains. But let us rejoice in knowing for those believers of Christ that our angels are where we want to be when our time comes.

ETHAN'S WINGS

Thank You Page

To my two earthly angels on loan, thank you for making my heartbeats worthwhile. Imani (Faith) you are my grace and Dominic you are my mercy. You give every breath that I take purpose. Thank you for choosing me to be your mom and allowing me to experience unconditional love. You love me when I couldn't love myself. I pray the hand of God continues to cover you for all of your days.

To Ernesto (Jacob), thank you for allowing me to be the mother of your children and being there through the ups and downs that these last twelve years have held. Enough credit does not go to you for the strength that you have had to endure through this loss. I pray for your continued strength and healing.

To my brother D.J, thank you for showing me what unconditional love looks and feels like. You accept and love everyone with open arms. To my mother Faye, thank you for showing me what hard work and determination can provide; to my father Melvin, thank you for being there for me when I call and showing me how to keep a smile in my heart. To Ernesto's mom Marina, thank you for showing me compassion in the midst of my sorrow and allowing me to see that God is the one who helps us heal in spite of our pain, no matter what our backgrounds are. Te Amo Mamita.

To my Zambrana family, thank you for your thoughts, your prayers, your tears, your laughs and most importantly your love to my family and I.

To my spiritual mother, my Pastor Dr. Denise Wilson, there are not enough thank you that I would be able to give you for what you have done for me and my children. This was a journey that my daughter and I traveled together in losing a loved one; but you have been guiding us along our spiritual journey. Without your spiritual guidance, this story would have remained silent; but this is a story where God gets all the glory, because He was the only one who held my hand.

We may not have walked on water with Jesus, but we would not have been able to survive that storm, if He was not holding our hand. Thank you for pushing me and helping me realize that my story was worth being told. To Sherita, Ratonya, Sarah, Nathalie, Vanessa, Vivette, Afua, Rev. Felicia Hawkins, Rev. Tracey Parris and so many others, thank you for your love and support and may God's grace continue to follow you for the rest of your days.

.

Table of Contents

Dedication.............................4

Thank You............................. 6

Forward...............................11

It began with a prayer....................13

He hears you............................19

Something just wasn't right..............22

It's in the blood........................25

It was my plea to Jesus...................29

His Salvation...........................33

I don't have my own strength...........38

How do you explain......................42

From your lips to God's ears............48

It's time...............................53

Trying again...........................57

We'll do this together....................60

Reassurance............................65

Fear and Faith.........................68

Obedience.............................75

Am I really alone.......................78

Reaffirming their bond...................85

Right now, right now....................89

His word is never void...................95

The promise.............................99

Conclusion..............................106

About the Author........................109

Forward

Loss is something that we all will face at one time or another, and each loss brings with it new emotions. Some of those feelings will catch us off guard, such as depression, confusion and becoming grief-stricken. And the truth of the matter is no two people will face the same emotions the same way in similar circumstances. But God has a way of dealing with us where we are and holding us close to him in the area of our hurt. Because of his infinite wisdom, we find that we end up stronger than when we started although sometimes not even knowing how we got there. That is what is meant by cast your cares on him because he cares for us. We can take that further; let him handle what needs to be tended too and just rest in the fact and faith that he already knows we will come out.

This book is a story of a journey of one woman's loss of a child. Now, this loss could have ended in self-destruction and giving up, but in the end, led to hope and promise. The loss of a child can be devastating, but if we trust that God knows best, we know it's not over, and we can go on. Go on this journey of hope and faith to new blessings and miracles. It will bless you tremendously.

Pastor Denise Wilson

The Rock Christian Center

Falls Church, VA

It began with A prayer

Genesis 25:21 NIV - Isaac prayed to the Lord on behalf of his wife, because she was childless. The Lord answered his prayer, and his wife Rebekah became pregnant.

I would hear her saying her prayers at night thanking God for another day; thanking him for her mommy and daddy and asking him for a little brother and sister. I shared with her dad the conversations that Faith and I had been having about her wanting siblings. Since she was getting older he thought that maybe it would be a good time to start trying, I looked at him and said, "I told her that this situation was between you and God." On one of the days that Jacob had to take Faith to her dance class, he asked her how everything at school was going. She said it was going okay, but a lot of her friends where having sisters and brothers. She couldn't understand why she didn't have one. He looked at her lovingly and said," something like that takes time honey"; she says well mommy says, "that it's between you and God," so you have to get on it daddy. He laughed and said okay, I'll see what I can do.

Well after a couple of weeks, I started not feeling well. I was nauseous, tired and just not myself. My coworkers would see me and say you don't look so well. They told me that I needed to go to the doctor to get checked. I was a little, apprehensive about going because if I were pregnant, then things would begin to change, but then reality set in because this was a lesson for me as well. A lesson in believing in what other people may pray for not just your prayer. Well, she began praying even harder as time went on and what do you know I was pregnant. Her father and I didn't tell her right away, we wanted to wait a little while, and we wanted to make it special for her. But after a couple of weeks of prayer, she shared that was beginning to have some doubts. One day after school on her way to an after-school activity, she started to cry. She had a look of sadness in her eyes that I had not seen before. I asked her what was wrong, and she said, "God doesn't hear me." With a puzzled look, I asked her "why do you think that?" She said, "Because I have prayed to God for a sister and brother and I still don't have one." With tears in my eyes, I wanted her to know that God hears you and He has heard you. I explained to her that the baby just doesn't come right away. The baby still has to grow inside the mother's tummy for some time.

By this time, I had gone to the doctor, and she had informed me that I was already six weeks along. A wave of excitement came over me, not only because I was pregnant, but because it was the first real test of the power of prayer for my daughter. We just had to figure out when was the best time to tell her. She was so faithful in her prayers that I wanted this to be a big deal for her because it indeed was. Her father and I discussed taking her to my next doctor's appointment, and that is how we would let her know that I was going to have a baby. We went to the store trying to figure out what things would be good for her on becoming a big sister.

We found a couple of books about mommy is expecting, and becoming a big sister. We also found a card and a couple of stuffed animals, one from us and one from the baby. We put everything in a gift bag and just anticipated being able to share this great news with her. I had a couple more weeks before my next appointment, so I was still trying to wrap my head around the idea of becoming a mom again. Some of my friends at work were trying to encourage me that it would be okay, that it was not like I had not done it before. I had so many emotions that I was feeling during this time; like how would I balance two kids, work, my daughters dancing schedule and trying to stay connected as a family. I questioned was I ready for this? Work was hectic during this time, and so was my daughter's dance schedule.

I was starting to become obsessed with work and trying to get as much work done as possible. I was questioning myself and God during this time. For some reason, I wondered whether I would carry this baby the whole time. I asked what I would do if it were a boy. I had no experience with boys, so in a sense, I was terrified. I was, scared to raise a young man during these times. I thought to myself. There are so many young men dying at the hands of each other and themselves. I wanted to believe that I was going to have another little girl, another little princess.

When my body would get tired, I would push myself a little bit harder, not giving myself time to rest. I struggled with when was a good time to let my supervisor know that I was expecting, but true to the spirit of the supervisor that I had during that time; she was very supportive and encouraging. I tried to convince myself that I wasn't pushing myself too hard. It was only a few days left for my next doctor's appointment, and I was getting excited. I imagined what it would be like for Faith and Jacob because it would be their first time seeing the baby. Our family as we knew it was changing, but it was a blessing we all were looking forward too and what my daughter had been praying about.

He hears you

**Psalm 66:20 - Praise be to God, who has not
rejected my prayer or withheld his love from me!**

The time had come for my appointment, and I was
excited because this would be the confirmation of what
my daughter had been praying for. This was the day to
let her know that even when you think God has not
heard you, He has, and He does things in His timing.
We went to my doctor's appointment that day and Faith
was wondering why she had to go to my appointment
and if she could go back with me. I told her that for the
first half of it, I would go back by myself, the nurses will
let you know when you and daddy will be able to come
back. After the nurse called me back, and my doctor
was starting to do the exam, I explained to her that
Jacob and Faith were in the lobby and today was the day
that we were going to let her know she was going to be
a big sister. I told her the story of Faith's prayer and

how this would be the moment that she would see that her prayers had been heard and answered.

I had brought along my camera because I wanted to capture this moment. After the doctor did the initial exam, it was time to see the baby. I had them bring Faith in, and I had the camera rolling. When she came in, the doctor began talking to her to make her comfortable. After everyone was comfortable, we started the sonogram. Once I knew she had a good view of the baby; I asked her if she knew what it was. She had this puzzled look on her face, but then she heard the heartbeat; so, I asked her again if she knew what it was. She nodded and began to cry. Then she fell into my arms, and we cried together. I whispered to her that he heard you and looked at me nodded and she smiled. Once the sonogram was complete, we gave her all her gifts. She looked in the gift bag and was so excited that all the books and stuff animals were all for her. Things continued normally for a while. I continued to work long hours some days. Other days were filled with drop-offs and pickups for Faith's dance classes. I was getting close to my 20-week checkup, and I began to fill uneasy like something was not right.

Something just wasn't right

Job 3:25 – What I feared has come upon me; what I dreaded has happened to me.

Things were about to change I just didn't realize how much. Jacob called me on a Monday night very upset, and I knew it had something to do with his job. I didn't panic, I just told him whatever it was God was going to see us through. When he came home he explained the situation with his job and revealed that he had been let go. But I had to believe as a family we would be okay. Having this situation come up with everything that had been going on was just a prelude of what was to come. I felt like I was just waiting for the other shoe to drop.

The next day we had a doctor's appointment to check on the baby. That uneasy feeling remained throughout the doctor's appointment. The baby just seemed sluggish. The doctor had a hard time getting the baby's heartbeat; but once she found it, everything looked fine. I went to work the next day, but I just didn't feel well all day. I felt tired and started to have pains, like heaviness in my lower stomach area. I tried to push through the day. I was even going to try and stay late that day, but the pain was getting worst. I went home and told Jacob that I wasn't feeling well. I thought about going to the doctor, but instead decided to try and lay down and get some rest. I was able to get a little bit of sleep, but the pain was coming and going. I was getting up every hour to go to the bathroom, which was not normal. I was starting to really get nervous and decided first thing in the morning I was going to call to make an appointment. But that opportunity never came.

At 11:30 pm my water broke, and I stood paralyzed with fear, because I knew there was no turning back. There would be nothing that they could do to change the outcome. I tried to wake Jacob without scaring Faith. When I woke him, I had such a look of terror on my face that he instantly knew something was wrong. I told him that my water broke, and I needed to get the hospital as soon as possible. Afraid for my health, he woke Faith in a hurry, so we could go to the hospital. She was scared and didn't understand what was going on.

It's in the blood

Ephesians 2:13 NIV– But now in Christ Jesus you who once were far away have been brought near through the blood of Christ.

She had asked me throughout my pregnancy how I would know when it's time for the baby to come. I had always told her when mommy's water break, this is the protection around the baby to keep it safe inside. Now that she knew the water wasn't there anymore, she also knew there was no protection for the baby anymore.

As we made our way to the hospital, Jacob ran a red light to try to get me to the hospital as quickly as possible. Unfortunately, there was a police officer nearby, and we were pulled over. I prayed that he wouldn't keep us long because I knew that I needed to get to the hospital quickly. When the officer asked for his driver's license, he explained "I'm sorry I ran the light officer, but my wife is in labor, and I'm trying to get her to the hospital. She's early." The officer gave him back his license and told him to be on his way. I tried to remain calm, but I knew that this moment would forever change not only my life but my family's lives as well.

When we finally made it to the hospital, I felt (relieved, afraid, anxious, etc.) As they were trying to check me in, the pains became stronger. They took me into to triage, and I had no idea of where my daughter was or where her father was. It seemed this was something that I would have to endure on my own. The nurse was trying to get me to undress so they could do an examination and something in her face change. She said, "We need to get you to lie down." "Just remove your bottoms," and something told me to look down. She was trying to keep my focus on her, and she kept talking to me; she told me not to look down. I looked, and the floor beneath me began to pool with blood. It was like someone turned on a faucet of water, but

26

instead of running water it was my blood. All I could do was call, "Jesus." Nurses and the doctor were coming from everywhere. They were trying to get me on the bed, so the doctor could get the machine to see where the baby was, but the pains were coming more frequently, and I could feel the baby coming. While the doctor was examining me more blood just kept coming. The nurse asked if I needed to push, but the doctor said no it would just come on its own, and with those words, the connection that I shared with this little person was no longer between us on the inside. Now it would show to others on the outside. The doctor caught my baby and said, "Ma'am it's a boy." My son took a breath, so he was alive.

The first nurse's attention was drawn to my small baby. She asked the doctor, "Shouldn't we be doing something?" "There is nothing that we could do," came his saddened reply. I didn't even get a close up look at my son. Instead, they went back to concentrating on me. With my son now born, they needed to get the placenta delivered. They had me pushing and pushing, but nothing but blood was coming. I was losing so much blood that they finally decided to go in and remove it for me. I had to quickly sign papers to give the authorization to put me to sleep so that they could do the procedure.

It was my plea to Jesus

2 Chronicles 6:19 NIV-   Yet, give attention to your servant's prayer and his plea for mercy. Hear the cry and prayer that the servant is praying in your presence.

I took those few moments when they gave me the anesthesia to plead the blood of Jesus. "I told God I understood that he needed my baby, but please don't take me away from my baby girl, she needs me, and I need her." With those words, I closed my eyes and drifted off to sleep. This sleep felt different though, it seemed much deeper, and I felt at peace. Sometime later they were trying to wake me in recovery; I was still really groggy. I struggled to wake from what felt like a deep sleep. I didn't want to wake; I just wanted to keep sleeping and imagine that this was just all an awful dream. As my eyes try to regain focus, I noticed with red eyes their dad looked at me and asked was I okay, because I looked so pale. He had never seen me look this way. He was so concerned with how I was looking; he asked the nurse "how much blood did she lose," that I needed two blood transfusions. The nurse explained that I had lost almost two liters of blood during the delivery process.

The nurse who had been with my baby asked if I had seen him, and I told her no, they took him so fast. She explained that she had taken pictures of him for me and if I wanted to see them. I took a deep breath and said "yes." I took the pictures in my hand and took my finger to trace his little face. He looked so at peace like he was just sleeping. I asked his dad if he saw the pictures, and that's when I found out, that while I was in the operating room, he was in the room with the baby. They began to explain to me that he lived for a little while and his dad was with him until his heart stopped. I knew he tried to hang on for a little while; he seemed like he was a little fighter. Once my blood levels were becoming normal again, they took me back to my room.

As I entered I noticed in the baby warmer area, he was still there. My little angel was still there. The nurse saw me peeking trying to see and asked if I wanted to see him and hold him. I wondered if I could hold him for a little while and she told me that I could keep him for as long as I needed to. As I pulled the blanket to

30

reveal his little face, I thanked God for allowing me to have this moment. He entrusted me with one of his most precious angels if only for a little while. I took in every inch of him from the five strands of sandy hair on his head to his little toes. I wanted everything about him etched in my mind. I took in every part of his being, the length of his fingers and toes, his weight, his father's nose, his small lips and his tiny ears. He was just this tiny being that had so much of an impact in such a short amount of time.

His Salvation

Psalm 62:1 NIV- Truly my soul finds rest in God; my salvation comes from him.

The nurse asked if we wanted the baby to have his last rights. Jacob is Catholic, but it was necessary to me that my baby's soul is given to God. When the priest arrived, she took the baby in her hands and asked what his name was; we had gone back and forth about what his name would be, and we looked at each other and said "Ethan," Ethan Jacob. In looking up the meaning of Ethan; it means firm, strong and Jacob means supplanter (to take the place of). But nothing could take the place of this special gift that I was given.

As she began to give Ethan his last rights, she spoke so beautifully and held him so gently, pouring from this little shell, water baptizing him and giving him back to Father. I remember feeling the sadness of not having him that long and having to give him back so soon. I looked at the whiteboard that was in the room and noticed the date that was there 9/24. I began to sob, and the priest wanted to know if I needed her to stop. Through my tears, I explained that I just noticed that the date was Jacob's birthday. What a way to celebrate the day of your birth with the death of your son. I apologized so much during that time because I felt like it was my fault. I was grieving knowing that he was never coming back, feeling as though I had somehow cheated him out of reaching his full potential and forever marking his Fathers day of celebration a day mourning.

My mind raced if I would have done something different; anything, maybe the outcome would not be what it is right now. At that moment I knew that this would affect many other people not just my family and me. Amid what was going on, I still needed to call my parents to let them know what was happening and to check on my daughter. Jacob's mom and brother had gotten my daughter off to school for us. I was able to get in contact with my dad, and through the tears, I let him know that I was in the hospital. It took a while to get in touch with my mom but explained that I was in the hospital and that I had lost the baby. I couldn't stand to repeat it, so I text one of my coworkers to let them know why I wasn't there and I would call the supervisor later. I had already left a voicemail stating that I would not be in and I wasn't sure when I would be back.

The motions of the day were running together. My dad was arriving and just trying to comfort me; another family member came in with face mask and gloves. Everyone was in there looking to see what the problem was. It was the time of the severe flu outbreak and nurses wanted to make sure that no one who was sick was on the floor. The nurse asked the person with the gloves and mask if they were okay and with a nasty tone, they responded, "do I look like something is wrong." I was like that is not called for, and you're the one coming in like you got the plague or something.

Mumbling under their breathe they just have the attention on them and just tried to cause problems during the time they were there.

They had other patients that they had to look after. But this was just the beginning of what was to come. The kids' other grandmother arrived and came in and wanted to make sure I was okay. She whispered to me that we would get through this together as a family and God would protect us. She asked if she could see the baby and I nodded. With her bible and rosary in her hands, she prayed over my baby, at that moment I saw that God would be the source of everyone's strength.

I don't have my own strength

Psalm 118:14 NIV-- The Lord is my strength and my defense; he has become my salvation

So as people began to leave and go on with their day, things were starting to happen quickly. I had to decide if I wanted to stay in the hospital for another day; what I was going to do with my child's remains, how was I going to explain this loss to my little girl, because she had prayed for this small miracle and now just like that, he was gone. How can you justify something to someone, when you don't even understand it yourself? God sent angels to surround me that day, to try and keep me in my right mind. Jacob and his mom left to go and try and make arrangements for Ethan. People were talking to me, but nothing was being received. I just nodded or shook my head in response to questions. I just wanted to close my eyes. How can you make burial arrangements for your child, who didn't get a chance even really to live?

With the room finally quiet for a little, I was able to spend a bit more time with Ethan before they took him away. I kissed him as many times as I could, and I held him as close to me for as long as I could, wishing he was still inside me. They had information and forms for me to go through. They wanted to know if I would authorize an autopsy on my baby. But he was so small; I told them "no he was fine the way he was." Someone asked me if I was sure, I told them "God gave him to me whole, and that is how I am giving him back." I told them the problem was with me and not him. As I was getting ready to leave the hospital, remembering what it was like to take Faith home, the realization set in when they brought me a box. The contents of the beautiful box made well up with tears, because I wasn't leaving the hospital with my baby in my arms, I was leaving with a box full of memories. Ethan's short life was summed up in a box. There was a poem that was provided for the loss of the baby from the hospital. A condolence card signed by all of our nurses, a little heart pillow, the hat that he wore after he was born, a sheet that he was covered with, cards with his name and footprints on them and his photo's that one of the nurses took.

I was released from the hospital later that morning and saw that clouds had started to clear, not knowing that it had been raining hard earlier. In retrospect, as my body began to pour blood in releasing my baby from my body, God opened up the heavens to receive his angel back to him with pouring rain. It was at that very moment that I felt my little angel had earned his wings. As I waited in the car for my prescription to be filled, it started to rain a little, and Whitney Houston's song came on "I Look to you." Through the tears, I remembered that music has always been my source of comfort for whatever I go through in my life. I took that as God's message and a reminder to look to him because I didn't have my strength to get through this. At that moment I realized that I was weak in my body, mind, and spirit. I was going to need to be strengthened in all those areas and more to make it through this.

How do you explain

Proverbs 3:5-6 NIV-- Trust in the Lord with all your heart and lean not on your own understanding; in all your ways submit to him, and he will make your paths straight.

After being helped in the house to lay down, my little girl came home not knowing what happened during the day. She just knew that I was back from the hospital and I needed to rest. She came in and gave me a great big hug and asked was I okay. I told her that I would be okay, it was just going to take some time. Her father and I went back and forth on whether to tell her. Losing her brother would be her first experience with death and how we approached it would remain with her forever. So, I prayed and asked God to give me the words to explain to her a situation that I didn't completely understand myself.

I was overwhelmed with the events of the last 24 hours, my emotions where all over the place. I was angry with myself because I felt if I had rested more and paid attention to the pains maybe things would have been different. Everything I did from this moment on I knew that I had to give everything over to God. I cried myself to sleep not wanting to wake up, but just praying for peace in my heart and my mind.

The next day, when my daughter came home from school, there was only one thing on her mind. She wanted to know how the baby was doing and when the baby was coming. It was then that I knew the time had come to tell her about the baby. I had to remind myself that I asked God to save me because she needed me. Now I needed him to strengthen me, so I could tell her the truth. So, I called her dad in and said to him that she wanted to know about the baby. Still hurt and trying to deal with his pain, he wanted to wait to tell her. But leaning on God, I knew in my heart that the time had honestly come. I had to tell her the truth.

She remembered hearing her dad tell his mom that my water had broken. She also recalled me telling her that the baby comes when the water breaks. I explained to her that my water did break, the baby arrived, and it was a boy, but we don't have him here with us here anymore. She looked at me puzzled. I reminded her of how she prayed for a sister or brother and that God answered her prayers when I became pregnant. But as we got closer to the time when he would come, God decided that he needed him more in heaven. So, her brother would now be a special angel that would watch over us from now on. With tears streaming from our eyes, she knew he was gone. She was heartbroken. She looked at me with such hurt in her eyes. "But I didn't get a chance to say goodbye, or hold him" she cried. She tried to understand why God would need her baby brother so much, but in her honesty, she said "he didn't want him as much as I did. I wanted him here with me for a very long time". At that moment as a family, we just held each other and cried.

The days became hard for me. I struggled to try and understand what had happened. I blamed myself and told myself that "if I would have lost more weight, got more rest, went to the doctor when I didn't feel right, then things would have been different. I had so many doubts in my head. I even asked God if this was my punishment for saying that I couldn't deal with having a little boy. Now I realized the truth was I didn't know how I could live without my baby boy. I didn't want to get out of the bed. I just wanted to keep my eyes closed and not wake up. My heart longed to be with my baby boy. But my soul was glad God had given me the chance to still be with my little girl. Jacob saw that I was struggling with my emotions and looked at me and told me that I couldn't blame myself because there was nothing different I could have done that would have changed the outcome of what happened. In my heart, I knew he was right and that I would have to accept God's decision. But I still struggled with my grief.

To make matters worse, I was faced with a situation that no parent should have to deal with during their lifetime. I had to decide how to bury my baby. It was during this time that I discovered how inconsiderate people could be. I was in the middle of trying to decide how to bury my baby, when a family member asked me, "When is the funeral for the baby?" Of all the things that they could have said at that moment, this was the worse. Why is it that when we go through our most difficult situations, people seem to overlook our feelings? I told them that we would not be having a funeral. That his father and I had decided the baby would be cremated; after all, no one wants to have to bury their child or make those types of arrangements. Instead of trying to understand how I felt or offering to help make arrangements for a memorial service, they began insisting on a funeral.

It was a lot of back and forth and was draining me more emotionally; I thought that this person would be a shoulder that I could lean on and instead, I distanced myself even more. I just couldn't deal emotionally and began to withdraw. I wouldn't accept phone calls from this person and would listen to the several messages that where left about a memorial service. I finally answered the phone, hoping that what I was going to say would be the last time that this issue was going to be addressed. I stated that our decision was still the same and that we would not be having a service; they were insistent that I give them a date because they needed to let their job know. And that's when I realized that it was never about needing to be there for my family and me, it was about what they would be able to get for themselves with my loss. I was so hurt, I told them to give your job any day you like so that you can have your days off from your job. I just couldn't believe that in my time of mourning that people would still try and take advantage of you and your situation. Not one time did this person while they had their time off come and visit nor did they offer help to my family. After seeing this, I had to go back to not accepting their calls for a while.

ETHAN'S WINGS

From your lips too, God's ears

Deuteronomy 29:4 NIV-- But to this day the Lord has not given you a mind that understands or eyes that see or ears that hear.

It wasn't long before I began to feel pressured to return to work. One manager called to ask how long I was going to be out. Again, my feelings were being overlooked. Nevertheless, I had been in the house for several days; so I decided to visit my job, just so a few people would know that I was okay. It took everything for me to find enough courage to see my co- workers and not break down in front of them. I was greeted with a lot of hugs and a few tears. The nurses from my doctor's office were advising me to take as much time as I needed to deal with what had just happened, but I knew no amount of time that I took off would ease the pain.

I only took off a week and a half after losing him. Some of my coworkers couldn't understand why I was back so soon, but I didn't have any other choice. I was the sole income provider for my family. I went back to working nonstop, they had overtime available, and I had plenty of work that needed to be caught up. One of my coworkers who I had become close too, looked at me with tears in her eyes and asked:" how can you do this"? I was little puzzled at first by what she meant, but she wanted to know how I had the strength to come into work every day with a smile on my face after experiencing such a loss. And I explained that it was only God who was providing me with that strength; I would love to be still pregnant and waiting for the birth of my baby, but I knew that was not going to happen. She looked at me and said "you are a strong woman. I don't know if I would have the strength to do what you are doing".

I then realized that this happened to me for a reason. I was not sure what purpose it would serve, but Ethan's death would not be in vain, and the pain would have some meaning. I worked almost nonstop. In not focusing in on the pain that I was in, I focused more on work and trying to improve myself. In my coworkers seeing what I was doing with my time, they began to open up to me about their own experiences with loss. I had young women with whom I had worked with three or more years and shared of their miscarriages and tried to give me encouragement that I could get through it. I saw the pain in some women's eyes that had been unearthed with my loss. I also had some people who were unsure of how to receive me or what to say to me.

There was a young lady that I spoke with every morning, and we talked about our families and our love for God. In not understanding her keeping her distance, I asked her how she was doing, and she started shedding tears and apologizing. Why are you apologizing to me? She stated that she had experienced a miscarriage a couple of weeks before I did and thought that somehow her experience had somehow contributed to mine. I looked at her and said; "with how much we love God and everything he has done for us, there was nothing that either of us could do to stop what happened and it was neither one of our faults." Losing our babies was all in God's plan; and even though we don't understand, it was meant to be this way. I told her, "but God is so good, what are the chances that he blesses us with another opportunity to get pregnant again and we go through that experience together." She looked at me and said, "from your lips to God's ears my friend." We embraced each other, and with tears in our eyes, and said, "we never know"; I continued to work like crazy, sometimes working ten to twelve hours, sometimes six days a week. Trying to balance between keeping things afloat at home with bills, time with my daughter, keeping up with work and feeling like my relationship with Jacob was kind of at a standstill.

In trying balance family time, I would work long hours during the day and on the days that Faith had dance class, I would sometimes pick her up. I used that time with Faith to do a pulse check to see how she was coping with things. Losing her brother was her first experience with death, but unfortunately not Jacob's first with someone who was extremely close too. Jacob remained distant and would go out at night for a couple of hours, but I just tried to give him his space. I guess I lived in a fantasy world thinking that our grief would bring us closer together, but it seemed we were growing further apart. We just didn't know how to comfort each other. Still, in my time of need, I was more worried about taking care of others and not focusing on myself.

It's Time

Genesis 18:10 NIV-- Is anything too hard for the Lord? I will return to you at the appointed time next year, and Sarah will have a son.

I worked like this for over a year. Once my workload had begun to improve I decided to try and work on myself with losing weight and getting some new clothes with bright colors instead of always dark colors as if I was hiding. My hard work was paying off. I received an award from my job; that is extremely hard to obtain, I had lost twenty pounds, and the clutter that had surrounded me that was my work was now gone. I decided that now I needed to take that same hard work ethic and use it to spend time with my family.

I needed to find a place where my family and I could have peace, a place where everyday life would have a new view for a couple of days. We found that place a couple of hours from where we lived. It was a beautiful beach with wild horses, wildlife and a view of the ocean where dolphins would appear. Chincoteague was a place where I closed my eyes and envisioned all of the nature talking with God. The waves of the water were the applause, the seagulls' calls were the roars from below, the flaps from the eagle's wings were whispers, and the dolphin's calls were them singing His praises.

I used that time to understand that as the waves come and go, so does grief in my loss. I had to learn how to allow myself to ride the waves of emotion, but not drown in them. It became vital for me to find beauty in everything that was going on around me like the laughter of family, or the cries of a single child. We all belong to God, and He created us in His image. We tried to enjoy every minute that we had with each other. Faith and her father played in the sand, went crabbing and as a family, we walked along the shore picking up seashells. As our mini vacation was ending, understanding that we would have to come back to reality was setting in, but with a different perspective. I

54

still had two people who loved and needed me so that they would become my focus.

I returned to work and developed a new strategy of how to approach my work. I set time frames for certain things to be completed throughout the day. The setting of timeframes allowed me to manage my time better and helped keep me organized. By developing strategies that helped me with my workload, it allowed me to help some of my other coworkers in reducing their workload and sharing some of my strategies with them. It's nothing like feeling like you are drowning, and no one is there throwing you a life preserver. I used those opportunities to encourage them that they could get out of their backlog and that there was light at the end of the tunnel. Having no backlog allowed me to be able to go home and spend quality time with my family. I wasn't focused on a workload, on how I was going to get through the next workday. I was focused on the here and now.

ETHAN'S WINGS

Trying Again

Psalm 26:2-3 -NIV- Test me, Lord, and try me, examine my heart and my mind; for I have been mindful of your unfailing love and lived in reliance on your faithfulness.

As Ethan's one-year anniversary approached, Faith came to me and said "mom, it's been a year already. Don't you think it's time to try again?" Surprised at her request, I looked at her as if I didn't know what she was talking about; but in my heart, I knew what she meant. "I don't know about that," I said. "I don't know if I'm ready to try again; I have to pray about it and talk to your dad." She looked at me with a smile on her face and said" "Mommy, you are the best mommy and I know that you can do it." I told her to pray about it too, and we will see what God and daddy have to say.

To be honest, I wasn't sure what to think about her request. Was I ready? Did I want to try again? What if the same thing happened again? I finally got up enough courage to sit down with Jacob and talk to him about the conversation that I had with Faith earlier in the day. He looked at me and said that he had been thinking the same thing but didn't want to pressure me. He felt the longer I took to try again, the less likely I'd want to try anymore. Still unsure, I asked if we could wait another year before deciding. But God has His timing for things. We just have to be willing to say yes. By December of the same year, my yes was being tested. I was feeling tired, and that friendly reminder that you are a woman was missing. I went to my doctor to get confirmation of what my daughter had been praying for and what I suspected was here sooner rather than later.

I looked my doctor and asked her if we were going to try this again. And she looked at me and said, this will be successful, but we will monitor you very closely. I was prayerful that we would not have me endure that pain again.

I kept the news of my pending pregnancy quiet for a couple of weeks. I needed to get used to the idea that God was going to give me another chance. This was the beginning of what He promised me the day I left the hospital over a year ago. I had to ride past that hospital every day on my way to work and back home. Those rides some days were a lot more difficult than others. Some days, I would have to pull off to the side of the road when I had a clear space because the grief that I was experiencing. On the better days, He would remind me that I would be back there but under happier circumstances. He promised me, so I had to trust what I couldn't see. I can't see God, but I believe him, he shows himself true every day when I can open my eyes.

We'll do this together

Hebrews 11:1-3 NIV-- Now faith is confidence in what we hope for and assurance about what we do not see. This is what the ancients were commended for. By faith we understand that the universe was formed at God's command, so that what is seen was not made out of what was visible.

In trusting him, I began to share the news with my coworkers and friends. Still, there was one friend that I had not seen in a while who I was desperately looking for. It was that young lady who over a year ago had experienced the same feeling of loss with losing her baby; just weeks before I lost Ethan. I went to her department to share the news with her. We greeted each other with hugs, kisses, and pleasantries. I asked her how she had been doing and she said that she was fine. I told her that I was looking for her because I needed to talk to her; I told her that I had to share some news with her. She stood there with a smile on her face saying, "I hope its good news." I had told her "remember a year ago the sadness that we had shared, and we talked about the goodness of God and as long as we believed anything is possible." I told her that I was expecting and with tears in her eyes she looked at me and said," me too." We had talked about our due dates and as before with our losses, the pending births where just weeks apart.

I laughed and looked at her and said remember in our sadness; I said that what if God gave us another chance to have another baby. What if he gave us another opportunity the experience would be so different. We would go through it together, and the results would be so much better. We hugged each other; cried and smiled because God showed himself true and our new journey together was just beginning. We would see each other during the weeks of our pregnancies and check in with each other to see how we were doing and to talk about God. In talking with her about God, we just couldn't help but thank him for all that He had done, what he was doing and what we believed he was going to do. We asked that he keep us through the journey.

On February 14th I had to go to a genetic specialist to have specific testing done. Since the doctors never knew what caused me to lose Ethan, they wanted to do genetic testing to make sure everything was okay with the baby. I was nervous because I was not sure of what was all involved with the testing, but I knew it had to be done. I went in to have my blood work done and as I am leaving; I see a familiar face, and it's my coworker who is currently pregnant. We never discussed having an appointment for the specific testing. We just looked at each other and laughed, because we were having to go through the same things and unknowing to us we were doing them together. We gave each other encouraging words as we went in for our ultrasounds to check on the babies. We hugged and told each other that everything would be fine. As I laid down to start the testing I prayed for my baby and hers, we had both endured enough at this point. The nurses where very kind and reassuring that everything would be okay.

They performed the exam and saw that everything seemed healthy, but we would have to wait for the results of the blood work. A couple of days went by, and I received a call from the genetics place. Everything with the baby was excellent, and all blood work was normal. Later that evening, I checked with my co-worker to see if she had received her call for her results. Everything with her results was fine as well. I continued working but made sure that any time that was being used for appointments, I made that time up. I went to the doctors' offices monthly, and everything seemed to be going well. I tried to make sure that I was drinking plenty of water and eating healthier. This time I wanted salads, fish, chicken, and vegetables. Not so much fast foods.

Every week my daughter and I would celebrate on a Tuesday because on that day the baby would be a week older and we survived another day, another week. We would thank God, every day but every Tuesday was our praise party. The weeks seemed to be flying by and with each checkup the baby seemed to be doing well, but that fear of something going wrong remained. We scheduled an ultrasound for 20 weeks, and that time we were to find out the sex of the baby. Up until now Faith just knew the baby was a girl but kept calling the baby "Chunky." I would tease her and tell her if it is a girl I don't think she is going to appreciate being called "Chunky." She would laugh and say it's just a nickname and I asked her would you want to be called that because you're a girl. She looked at me and said I guess not; but with all honesty, she said: "can I just continue to call the baby that until we find out what it is, I like the name."

Reassurance

Genesis 50:21 NIV-- So then, don't be afraid. I will provide for you and your children." And he reassured them and spoke kindly to them.

The calendar had been marked and with nervousness, the day had come for my 20-week ultrasound. This was a very trying time for me because I had prayed that we would make it to this day and beyond and we were halfway there. Reassurance came when I was able to see this little face appear on the screen. We checked to make sure that bones where forming correctly, that all the organs were functioning properly. I could gather that while the test that was being performed, this baby did not like having its private space invaded. The technician would go to look at one part of the body to check something and the baby would either kick or move altogether. It didn't want to be pressed on; poked at, looked at, or bothered.

When it came time to find out the sex of the baby, the technician laughed and said I guess it wants to be difficult today. It's balled up like a little bunny rabbit and doesn't want to be seen. I just smiled, because that meant determination was there, and a fighter was in there. The baby had been through enough, so we called it a day. I remember going home that day and laughing with my daughter because she wanted to know what the sex of the baby was, and I couldn't tell her because now it was a little bunny rabbit.

I would have to wait a few more weeks to have another ultrasound. I tried to make sure that I got plenty of rest, ate healthier and walked more, but I started experiencing pain in lower abdomen when I would sit for long periods of time and then try and get up. I went and bought a seat cushion for work, to see if that would help. My job even ordered a special footrest for me to try and help with relieving the pressure that I was having.

That feeling that something wasn't right was coming back. But I was reminded that God made a promise to me. I just had to continue to believe and pray that we both would be okay. Each week the pain would get worse, and I kept telling myself that I just needed to make it until August 30th the baby's due date. I didn't want to tell anyone the pain that I was in because I didn't want to seem like I was complaining; it's called pregnancy. Everyone experiences some aches, some pain, and discomfort during pregnancy; I just needed to make sure I didn't dismiss it if the pain got worse.

Fear and faith

Psalm 52:8-9 NIV-- But I am like an olive tree flourishing in the house of God; I trust in God's unfailing love for ever and ever. For what you have done I will always praise you in the presence of your faithful people. And I will hope in your name, for your name is good.

After four more weeks of anticipation, the day had come for my doctor's appointment and ultrasound. I was excited because I knew this would be the day when we would find out what we were having. But of course, this would not be a typical day for the doctors. I arrived for my regular appointment, and my blood pressure was up a little. I was spilling more protein in my urine, but it was the same thing with the other two pregnancies, so this was not a shock to my doctor, she just knew what to try and focus on more to get my numbers to be as normal as possible. It was time for me to go downstairs for my ultrasound and my nerves were all over the place. Since they were running behind, I used the time to refill my bladder with water so that we could run the test. As we started the test, everything was going well.

The baby was stubborn as usual because it didn't want to be bothered. I asked the baby to behave so that we could find out what it was. When we came to the part to find out what the baby was, he decided to cooperate. Yes, I said he, it was another boy. God had given me another chance; I knew that Ethan could never be replaced, but he wanted me to see that it didn't matter if it was a girl or boy it was a blessing that He had entrusted me with to birth.

The appointment was taking longer than usual, so I started to get nervous because I knew that there was something wrong. The sonographer reassured me that everything was fine with the baby, but something did not appear normal with me. After several checks by the technician, the supervisor was called in to examine me.

They discovered that my cervix had started to open from the inside, and had opened to the point that I had to see my physician right away. My heart sunk because I was in fear that the same thing that happened to Ethan was now getting ready to happen to this baby. My doctor informed me that the opening in my cervix was serious enough that I had to go to the hospital that day. I cried so hard for an hour because He promised me that the same thing would not happen again and from my view of things I was very close to it being that way. But looking back on it now, I understand God was working it out in my favor. He had them do a detailed look, and they found what was wrong, saving me from the same fate as before.

I had to go home and pack a bag for a couple of days because they did not know how long I was going to be in the hospital. I had to try and explain to Faith that I had to go to the hospital so that they could watch over her brother and I. It was to take care of us and to make sure that my cervix had remained the same and had not opened further. Having to go back to the hospital at this stage in my pregnancy brought on anxiety for Faith and I because we did not know what would be found when we got there. She cried so hard on the way to the hospital that I wanted to cry myself. Instead, I had to remain calm in front of her and tell her that everything was going to be okay. I would be back home; I just didn't know how long that was going to be. With my dad in the back seat with her, he consoled her by allowing her just to express her feelings. My dad was great in explaining to her, that this was a good thing because I was in a place where they would able to check to make sure nothing was wrong, and if there were a problem, it would be easier for them to do something.

When we arrived at the hospital, and I was registered in, I tried to take a moment with her before I was taken to my room and I prayed with her. We prayed that everything with her brother and I would be okay and that I would be home soon. We hugged and kissed once more before I was finally taken to my room.

I had to share a hospital room with a roommate who had a lot of company. They were kind of loud, so I decided to pull out my iPod and listen to some gospel music. Music has been my source of comfort my whole life. It has helped me through new loves found and loves loss. I changed my clothes and had to get ready for all of the tests that they were getting ready to do on me. They had to do blood and urine work; hook the baby and me up to the monitor to make sure that he was still moving and to make sure I was not contracting. After all the test where done, they had to elevate the bed with my feet being higher than normal. My bed had to be elevated so that pressure would be taken off my cervix, reducing the chance of my cervix opening further.

I prayed and cried all night because I wanted to be home with my baby and I was not sure how long I was going to have to stay there. As fear set in, I began to try to bargain with God. I told God that if he let me go home and not have to remain in the hospital, that I

72

would do whatever he told me to do, whatever the doctors told me too. The following morning, I had breakfast, more blood work was done, they did more monitoring of the baby, and I had to endure another exam to check on my cervix again. When they came with a wheelchair to take me for an ultrasound; I was nervous. But I had to settle myself and pray that things would be better.

The technician was friendly, and she explained everything that she was about to do. She checked the baby to make sure he was okay, and he turns and opens his legs to show, see I'm a boy. I just laughed and said to the screen "we see you, " and I see a motion of his hand as if he waved. That was my reassurance that he was okay. The technician laughed and said, "he is a flirt already." She continued the exam and checked my cervix. In reviewing my cervix, you could still see the opening, but the images had to be reviewed by the doctor who was on call for that day and with my regular doctor. After a few hours of waiting, the doctor who was on call came to go over the results with me. It seemed that things had remained the same, but I would still need to be monitored closely. The doctor explained that since I was, further along, I would not need a medical procedure that they sometimes do to keep the baby in until term. Within a few more hours, my doctor finally stopped by after making her rounds. She said she would release me from the hospital and she would see me in her office the following week. Because of the results of the exam, she didn't want me returning to work. Instead, I would spend the remainder of the week at home.

So, I contacted my supervisor to inform her that I would not be in for the remainder of the week and after a follow-up appointment, I would be able to give a better idea of when I would be back. I stayed in bed for the rest of week and weekend. I was able to catch up on some sleep, but just thinking about having to be in bed was a little daunting. While I was hopeful that I would be able to go back to work soon, I remained prayerful that my baby and I were okay.

Obedience

Psalm 128:1 NIV-- Blessed are all who fear the Lord, who walk in obedience to him.

As my doctor's appointment approached a sense of nervousness came over me again. I went to the doctor's office and completed another exam to see if there was any change in my cervix. In reviewing the images, she was able to see that there had been a slight change and was concerned that I would have to remain on bed rest for another two weeks. I just couldn't wrap my head around not being able to go back to work, not being able to drive and having to be in the house. But this was the beginning of my test of putting my trust in God. Remember in the hospital I bargained with God that if he let me get out of the hospital, I would do whatever he and the doctors told me to do. See when I became pregnant again, I had to make that decision if I wanted to change doctors. But I had to get out of my feelings and understand, that in losing Ethan it didn't just affect my family and me that in some way it had to affect my doctor also. She lost a patient that day, and it had me think, what had that loss done to her spirit? She reviewed all my tests when I lost him because she wanted to make sense of loss for herself and me.

She didn't have any answers at that time, and I told her that it had to be that way, it was God's will. When I became pregnant again, she was excited and asked was I ready to do this again. But, was I ready; I had to decide after I found out that I was pregnant again about if I wanted to keep the same doctor. Memories that we had shared came flooding back to me. She made the pregnancy reveal of Ethan so special. She played such an important part of our lives that I couldn't be on this journey without her. I was doing this again, and she was a part of this journey also. She made sure that she went over everything with the baby every time she did my exam. She wanted better results than the last time. The determination for her was there; I had to trust that she

77

wanted this pregnancy to become a fruition as much I did.

She looked at me with all seriousness and said that I need you be to on bed rest for another two weeks, I need the pressure off your cervix, this is what is keeping this baby inside. If you are not going to remain in the bed, then I would have to send you to the hospital so that you can be monitored during this time. I just did not want to be in the hospital at all until it was time to have him. I contacted my supervisor again to inform her of what was going on. She wanted to make sure that I was okay and reassured me that my job was secure. My job right now was to take care of myself and my baby. She gave me the information to contact personnel on the job so that the proper paperwork could be filed for my short-term disability. This was about me being obedient to what I was being asked to do. This was me realizing that I was not in control of anything at this point. I was not in control of my job, my body, or my situation. I could only control my

prayers.

Am I really alone

Deuteronomy 31:8 NIV- The Lord himself goes before you and will be with you; he will never leave you nor forsake you. Do not be afraid; do not be discouraged.

My faith was getting ready to be tested yet again. After being on bed rest for almost a month already, my doctor reviewed my results and informed me that I would be visiting her office every week, but remaining on bed rest. But strict bed rest; I had to lie on my side, I could not sit up to eat, watch T.V. or do anything. I could only get up out of bed long enough to use the bathroom, and I had to go right back to bed. This meant that I had to be solely dependent on someone else. She explained that I would need to come in to see her once a week to get my exam for the baby and I and the following week I would come in to see the nurse. I would see the nurse so that she could administer a shot in my sides to try and help prevent me from going into labor.

I would have to lean on God even more because the behavior of someone that I depended on the most was becoming questionable. I was left at home on a Saturday morning by myself with only receiving breakfast. I was a little taken aback, when the afternoon came around, and no one was still home. I began to cry with frustration because I was starting to think that this was going to be happening to me more often. It was frustrating because I didn't ask to be placed on bed rest nor did I ask for a complicated pregnancy. I don't think the seriousness of the situation was realized; this could be potentially life or death for the baby. I called my dad crying, and I explained the situation to him of what had recently happened. He had been to my home off and on to check on me and Faith to make sure we were okay. He explained that he would be out at my house on Monday to see what he needed to do. My dad is a pistol at times and what you won't do is treat his baby and his grandbaby anyway. For that remainder of that day, I had to get up and try to fix myself lunch and dinner. Faith and Jacob did not come home until later that night. My dad called the next day after he had gotten home from church to check on me and he wanted to know what time they got back home and after I told him what time you could hear the anger in his voice. After that, I knew Monday was going to be a revelation for someone.

My dad arrived Monday morning, and I just cried when he came in to hug me. I had not felt that alone in a long time. My dad called Jacob into the room with all seriousness and a few cuss words mixed in and asked if he wanted to be here or not. The situation that I was in was not a pretend situation that I was not lying in bed because I wanted to, but I was there because I had too. This was being done to try and help to save my babies life, so I would not have to experience that type of loss again. At first, he wanted to play it off like he didn't know what my dad was talking about. But my dad was not in the mood for any games; he asked him "what I ate for lunch and dinner for the last two days?" He couldn't tell him what I had since he wasn't there. Jacob responded, "that he was here, and it wouldn't happen again." He wasn't happy that I got my dad involved, but I was doing what was best for my baby and me.

My dad has always been the type of man that if he has it; it's yours, don't get me wrong, he is not perfect, but who is expect God almighty himself. One thing has always remained true, and that was that he loved my brother and me, and now that I was having children of my own he loved them just the same if not more. After his conversation, my dad came to me with his love and asked me what I needed him to do. "If you need me to come and stay with you to make sure that you and my grandbaby are alright, I will do it." He worked at night so that he would be home with me during the day. For a couple of days, everything seemed okay.

There was still tension between Jacob and me because now trust was being questioned. It was that question of when he left the house, was he going to use that time to have his alone time and not come back for a while. It was difficult to see where Jacob's head was at; there was little conversation between us. I remember feeling so much sadness. Because here I was given another chance to be a mom again and it felt like resentment was starting to play a role in our lives, but maybe it wasn't resentment at all, but the fear of the unknown. Fear of having to lose another child or even me; could this be the reason for the behavior; I just didn't know.

My dad would see that I was struggling and beginning to stress over the situation, so he remained at the house with me. My dad would come home in the morning after working overnight and would make sure that I had breakfast, Jacob would make sure that I had lunch and dinner. During this time, I tried to convey, that I appreciated everything that Jacob was doing. Because it was a lot of responsibility, having to wait on me hand and foot, taking care of our daughter, taking her to school, picking her up, taking her to dance class and having to go to work at night, but it's life and people do it every day.

I felt so isolated and alone; I found myself becoming more withdrawn. This was a hard time for everyone and emotions where high. I just knew that I could only try and control my feelings and it was important that I handled things very carefully. I started to use this time to focus on myself and the baby. I promised myself that after I had this baby, that I would find a church that the kids and I could attend.

I was beginning to feel the need to be closer to God, and I needed to be somewhere that I could be nurtured. I had always had a belief in God, and I was able to see the power of prayer first hand from my grandmother. My dad's mom was the type of woman, who when you saw her, you saw the acts of God. If you were hungry she fed you, if she saw that you needed clothing, she gave it to you. If she saw a need, she didn't wait for you

85

to ask, she went ahead and made things happen. I'm sure times were hard, but you would never know because she always seemed to have more than enough.

When I would spend the summer with her for a couple of weeks, I would see her on her knees before she went to bed and she would get up early in the morning and be on her knees again praying. Sunday mornings were always special for me because that meant that more family members would be coming over for breakfast, but more importantly, before breakfast, we would have family prayer. Everyone would find a space on a couch, chair, step or corner and everyone from the babies to the adults would be on their hands and knees praying and saying a bible verse. I was feeling so alone at times, that I felt that the only one that I could go to was God, I had to cast all of my cares on him, talk to him and cry out to him. I could feel myself going into a downward spiral, longing to feel closeness from my partner but instead feeling like this was how things were going to be from here on out. This when I would draw on those memories of my grandmother because I knew she had prayed for me and was now in heaven with Ethan watching over me.

Reaffirming their bond

2 Corinthians 2:8-9 NIV-- I urge you, therefore, to reaffirm your love for him. Another reason I wrote you was to see if you would stand the test and be obedient in everything.

The bond that was starting to form between Faith and the baby was special. The love I have for this little girl was reaffirmed even more when after a doctor's visit and receiving one of the shots, she saw that I was in pain and did not want to leave me alone. Since her dad worked at night, it was just her and I home alone. She asked about the shot and why it was so painful. I explained to her that since I had to go to the doctor every week, there was a lot involved. I would have to be assisted to get in and out of the car since it had been such a long time with me being on bed rest. If I stood for long periods of time, I would feel pressure, so I would have to be in a wheelchair from the time I arrived at the appointment until it was time for me to leave. I explained that the medicine was an oil base medicine and it burned when they stuck me with the needle. The pain was more evident because I couldn't sit up in the bed; all I could do was lay on my side and when I had to lay on the side where I received the shot it was almost unbearable. I was receiving the shots every other week, so by the end, the nurses felt so sorry for me because I was developing scabs. I would look at the scabs and just think about how much pain I was in, but I wanted to remember the pain because it was my reminder that the baby and I were still here. When I would get frustrated about having to be in bed and wanted to cry and say I couldn't do this anymore, I tried to remember that pain of not having Ethan; reminding myself, that this pain had a purpose. The pain that I was enduring this time was for my gift.

This pain I had to go through was to ensure what God had promised me was not forgotten. I could still put my hand on my stomach and know that he was still there, I could still feel him move, and it was my reminder that it could have been the other way. I understood that I had to appreciate this experience because He didn't have to allow me to have another chance at having another baby. Never doubt what God has for you, every experience has its purpose. Whether it is a lesson learned; a test of your faith, a new walk on a corrected path or him grabbing your attention, it's all in his will. He gives these trials or test as some may say to remind us that he is still God and that he is still there.

These weekly doctors' visits lasted from twenty-five weeks until I was thirty-six weeks. I had tried to stay positive throughout this whole process. Even with being home, I still had hopes of going back to work before I had him. My doctor finally gave me clearance to go back to work on August 4th. I was so excited that I could go back to work that I contacted my supervisor to let her know. She was happy to hear from me, and she understood my excitement about wanting to come back to work, but she remembered everything that I had been enduring. She reassured me that my job was secure, but wanted me to remain home to be on the safe side. Her fear was me coming back to work and having him there on the job. I stayed home, but things changed sooner than I thought they would.

Right now! Right now!

Romans 8:24-27 NIV-- For in this hope we were saved. But hope that is seen is no hope at all. Who hopes for what he already has? But if we hope for what we do not yet have, we wait for it patiently. In the same way, the Spirit helps us in our weakness. We do not know what we ought to pray for, but the Spirit himself intercedes for us with groans that words cannot express. And he who searches our hearts knows the mind of he Spirit, because the Spirit intercedes for the saints in accordance with God's will.

On August seventh I celebrated my birthday at home and just waited for the time for his arrival. Faith was hoping that he came on my birthday, so there would be a bright spot for my birthday, unlike her dad's birthday. I told her he would choose the day that he wanted to come. She looked at me and said," I just want one of you guys to have a happy birthday"; she thought that her dads birthday would always be sad since her brother's death was on Jacob's birthday. I explained to her" that birthdays are a celebration of life." Even though he is not here with us, we still celebrate him; he will forever be apart from our lives and in our heart. Although he was here only for a little while we honor the gift that he was and is. We try and light a candle for him every day. We also placed a live plant next to his urn as a way to honor his life; it was a beautiful plant that was given to us by Faith's dance group.

Trying to understand, that to be absent from the body, is to be present with the Lord. With the pending birth of another baby boy, I couldn't help but wonder what he would have been like, who he would have looked like, how he would have been with his sister and with his baby brother. I was a little sad because I missed him so much, but was filled with joy knowing that Ethan's passing has allowed for the new baby to come. Faith was beginning to get into the swing of things,

93

since school had already begun. Faith was still sleeping in the bed with me because she did not want to leave me alone and I had started to sleep with towels in the bed because of a scare the week before. Faith would have water bottles on the bed, drinking them before she would go to bed or wake up thirsty. One morning she was getting ready for school, and I was lying in bed, and I felt something wet pooling underneath me, I thought to myself, that this could not be possible. I started to panic a little bit, but something told me to check to see if I could tell what it was; the side of my nightgown was wet, and when I went to smell it, it smelled like grape something. Looking around on the bed, I found that she had left a flavored grape bottle of water from the night before. From that moment on, I began to sleep with something underneath me.

On a Tuesday morning, at 6:30 I was watching the news getting ready to wake Faith up for school when there was a warm gush of water. I laid there for a minute wondering could this be it, he had just turned 37

94

weeks. I told Faith "my water just broke"; she sat up on the bed quickly with big eyes and said, "right now, right now." Laughing I said right now, right now; she jumped up with a rush saying, "Oh my gosh what do I do, what do I do?" She had a look of fear and excitement on her face. I looked at her and told her she would first need to calm down, I asked her to get me some towels to put on the floor by the bed, so when I stood, the water wouldn't get all in the carpet. In preparing for the new baby's arrival, we had the carpet replaced, and his crib was put together just the days before. We were home alone, and her dad was late coming in from work. I tried to reach him on my cell phone several times, but I was having issues with my cell phone calling random numbers or not calling the number that I needed at all. Of course, this morning was no different.

All I had was my little girl who was trying to help me pack for the hospital. I was becoming more and more frustrated because I couldn't reach Jacob, so I decided to try to reach my dad. He was already on his way home

95

when I called, and I explained that I needed him to get in contact with Jacob because my water had broken, and I needed to get to the hospital soon, and my phone was still acting up.

My dad was a little upset because he wasn't home yet, and my daughter and I were home alone. Jacob finally called asking what was going on, your dad called and said your water broke. Are you okay, are you in any pain were his next questions? I asked where he was, and he was on his way home, but driving on the highway in rush hour traffic in our area proved a little challenging that morning when rushing, and he missed the exit to get to our house. But what could I do, all I could do was wait. After redirecting my attention back to my daughter, I told her to get dress for school and make sure everything is together in your book bag. After she had everything done, I did her hair for school, and she finished putting my things together that I needed for the hospital when her dad walked in the door. He walked in the door asking what was going on; your dad said something about your water breaking. I stood up out of the bed so that he could see for himself that my water had broken. I felt calm knowing that my miracle was on his way.

They helped me get dressed, and we had one of our neighbors to take Faith to school. He pulled the car up and loaded the bags into the car. After helping me in the car, I saw my dad coming around the corner after getting off the bus. I told him to come on; we had to go. He started laughing saying going where I thought by the time I got here you would be gone. I looked at him; laughed and said, "Well I guess you didn't time it right, get in the car we have to go." I love my dad, even in a moment of panic he still knew how to calm me down and make me laugh.

His word is never void

Numbers 23:19--20 NIV- God is not a man, that he should lie, nor a son of man, that he should change his mind. Does he speak and then not act? Does he promise and not fulfill I have received a command to bless; he has blessed, and I cannot change it.

I arrived at the hospital on August 9th at 7:45 am and was checked into triage as soon as I arrived. I was calm and had no pain at all. I remained in the triage for a couple of hours waiting for a room to become available. During the time in the triage, I began to remember the last time I was here and the terror that I was feeling. The feeling of hopelessness that there was nothing I could do to change things, but looking at what God had promised me and knowing that his word was not void. I remembered being in triage to only be a few spaces away, from when my world felt like it had ended; just to begin again with the birth of the new baby. I was able to lay there and labor with no pain and by the time I got to my room, I was 4 cm dilated. I was still comfortable, so

I asked to get my epidural, so that I could remain comfortable. The labor was slow, but I was still progressing. Jacob was hoping that he was going to come that same day because it was his grandmother's birthday. I told him that would be nice, but he was going to choose when he wanted to come. The epidural had finally been placed, but only to realize that it just took on one side of my body.

I didn't want it to be taken out and put back in again, so I had to just deal with the pain. My dad and mom had been there all day, so I asked my dad to go home, it was going to be a while before he would come, and he had already been up all night. We had worked it out with Jacob's mom and brother that my Faith would stay with them and they would take her to school the following day.

It was already after 10:30 pm, and he was still taking his time, I had finally reached 9 1/2cm, and my mom was ready to go home. Jacob was going to take her

99

home, and when they got to the parking garage of the hospital, she felt bad because if she had him take her home, I would be by myself. And my mom didn't want him to miss the birth of his son. This would be a full circle moment for Jacob, for on this day he would have the memory of seeing another son take his first breath of life and not just the memory of seeing his first son heart beat for the last time. It was a day of revelation that God saw our pain individually and together; but through it all, he made way for all of us. As I got closer to the 10 cm I was able to feel a little pressure; I knew that I could begin to push. With every push, God's promise was coming closer to be a reality. Unlike my birthing experience with Ethan; before he came, the blood that flowed from my body was like living water.

It was what connected me to him, as I pleaded with God to spare my life and now with the pending birth of the new baby John 7:38(Whoever believes in me, as Scripture has said, rivers of living water will flow from within them). In that moment of losing a child I sought

God and going through this challenging pregnancy he remained ever present, in birthing this new baby, it was peaceful.

The promise

2 Corinthians 1:20-22 NIV- For no matter how many promises God has made, they are "Yes" in Christ. And so, through him the "Amen" is spoken by us to the glory of God. Now it is God who makes both us and you stand firm in Christ. He anointed us, set his seal of ownership on us, and put his Spirit in our hearts as a deposit, guaranteeing what is to come.

Finally, at 1 am, a little face appeared screaming. This time the tears that fell were tears of joy. I was able to share this moment with my mom and Jacob. I was able to hold him in my arms and look into his eyes and see that Gods promises are true. After cleaning him off, they took him over to check his vitals. He seemed to be fine, but after a few minutes, his breathing became labored. They were concerned enough to call the neonatal doctor on duty at that time. She came in to check on him, and I told her that he is a stubborn little one. She looked at him and monitored his responses from the test she was conducting. Everything seemed fine except his breathing did seem a little labored to her as well. She attempted to have him cry so that she could check to see how much air he was able to intake.

I began to pray because we had endured everything during the pregnancy with faithfulness knowing what God had promised would one day become true. I asked God to keep him and watch over him; I plead the blood of Jesus over him because his promise does not come back void. She was finally able to tap him on his bottom and get a good cry from him. She looked at him and said that he was getting enough air into his lungs and he seemed to be fine. I was still a little concerned but was quickly reminded, that when you give things to the Lord, you have to leave it there and let his will be done. I was starving during this time, and since it was so early in the morning, all I could get to eat were some graham cracker and apple juice. I just tried to enjoy the moment and thought of it as nourishment for my body, since I was nursing.

After he was checked and given back to me, I looked him over and took in everything about him. Here was my promise in the flesh, my faithfulness was being rewarded. Once we got to my room, the nurses were able to find me a sandwich and some graham crackers and apple juice. They took the baby to get him cleaned up and to allow me a couple of hours of sleep before his next feeding. I used the time that I nursed him as our bonding time. I just looked at how beautiful I thought he was and thanked God for giving me another chance.

They wanted me to get up out of bed and move around since my epidural was starting to wear off when the baby was not in the room. It was hard to move around in the beginning; I still had some numbness in my leg from my epidural wearing off. I would have this numbness for weeks after I had him. The nurses were extremely helpful. They took great care of me and

104

helped me with the baby. Later that day I was scheduled to be released from the hospital, and I was ready to go home. We had to decide on this little guy new name we looked at him and said, Dominic Elijah. Dominic means "to belong to God, " and Elijah means "the Lord is my God," how fitting a name for a little boy, who by only God's grace was able to come into existence. Because he had gotten his pictures taken earlier that morning, he was dressed and ready to go. As we waited for Jacob to come back; I thought about what that moment would be like for Faith. You see with the death of Ethan she never got a chance to hold him or see him in person, but now with Dominic, she had the opportunity to have a new memory added. She was able to be rewarded for her faithfulness in believing in the power of prayer. Allowing her to see that he heard her; prayers and the emptiness that she felt in losing her brother did not go unnoticed.

God was now going to replace that emptiness with arms full of love. When Faith arrived at the hospital with her dad, she gave me lots of hugs and kisses. She was able to see her brother and hold him finally. That moment was when I realized that the one thing that she wanted with the loss of her brother, she was now able to have another brother's embrace. And all because of her faithfulness in trusting God with her prayers. After holding him for a while, she looked at me and said, "mommy you did a great job." You can go ahead and have another baby. I looked at her and said, "What did you say"? She looked at me with all smiles and said, I would like a sister. I informed her that we should probably get her brother home first before we continue talking about other babies. This was her proof of the power of prayer. He is faithful and true if you believe.

Recently, Faith posed a question to her dad about wishes. She asked him; if he had to choose between two wishes, which one would he choose. She asked him "would you want to go back home to your native country by yourself for a year or do something that you've always wanted to do"? He looked at her and said,

106

"that is not fair he said; I want four wishes." He then began to explain his four wishes to her. First, I want to meet your mom all over again; then I want to watch you be born again, next I want to have more time with your brother Ethan because the time was not long enough and finally to watch your brother Dominic being born again.

In listening to the conversation, it gave me an opportunity to a have a reflective moment with Faith. I shared with her that her father and I had two different experiences with the loss of her brother. I was able to develop a bond with Ethan for five months because he was growing inside of me. I was able to feel him move for the first time, was beginning to notice the signs in my body when he was hungry or tired.

And I realized at that moment, that her dad's experience was different but that he was just as important. I was able to build and share my love for him from the very beginning of his life and the nurture and care I was able to give him from the inside of my body. But the love and care that his father was able to give him at the end were just as valuable. He took his first breath with me there and held on for quite some time with his father watching his heartbeat until it completely stopped. But what a gift from God that it was his father that was there to be with him at that moment. It allowed me to share with my daughter that is how God is there with us. He is there with us from the very beginning before we are knitted in our mother's wombs, how he handpicks us from heaven and places us in our mother's arm.

But in having her father there with her brother, it represented that as we take our first or last breathe that God is always there. Through our transitions of life; losing a loved one, getting married, giving birth, going away to college, accepting God as your Lord and Savior that he is right there holding our hands and guiding us.

Conclusion

In looking back in writing this story, it is my prayer that sharing my story will allow someone who is grieving the loss of a child or loved one to know that they can continue to live. Though it is challenging to deal with the loss of a loved one, we must not die in the process. We have to realize that we must live; live to see what God has planned for us to have. I had my moments of wanting to give up and not going on, but in writing this story it made me think back on many times we were so close to our blessing, but we gave up too soon. How many of you have even taken that leap of faith and listened to the steps that God has ordered? When he told you to go to a particular place at a certain time, and you wanted to go your way, at the time. That assignment that you passed on could have been your blessing or someone else's blessing. They didn't receive their blessing because you didn't complete your assignment. Trusting God in what He is trying to give us, is the ultimate test. Saying yes to his will is just like you signing your name for the test, but that's just the beginning. What are you willing to do for God? He shows us daily that anything is possible if we allow him to lead us. Ethan has earned his wings, and I pray his story was able to soar to each of your hearts.

I would like to also like to encourage the reader who has never experienced this type of loss but just wants to know of ways to address people who have. There are no comforting words that can be given at the time that would truly help in easing their pain. Just being present for them will be of help and seeing what their needs are. Allow them to express themselves in whatever phase of their grief that they are in as long as it is not harmful to themselves or someone else. Ask them what they need, keep them in prayer and remember them months and years down the line. Everyone's grieving process is different, and some grieve longer than others. Please show compassion and love to those who have lost a loved one.

ETHAN'S WINGS

About the Author

KiKi Jones is a Christian author; mother of three, one of which has earned his wings. She lives in VA with her two spunky, creative children who are both school age. As a first-time author, it was pain and silence that caused her to tell her story. After losing her son, she encountered many friends and family members who had suffered the loss of a child but remain silent. Their silence was deafening when the pain resurfaced.

KiKi didn't want that to be her and Ethan's story. She used that pain to propel her into authorship. After losing her son she looked for something that could help her in her grief and she could not find what she was looking for. Losing her physical baby made a way for new babies (her books) to be birthed. She is currently working on another project. When KiKi is not working on a new project, she enjoys finding new creative activities that she can do with her children.

If you would like to reach out to KiKi Jones, she can be reached on her Facebook page Authors Page KiKi Jones.

.

ETHAN'S WINGS

Made in the USA
Middletown, DE
04 March 2018